TWINS

TWINS

A Unique World Scenario

Jørgen Lyngbye, M.D., Ph.D.

VANTAGE PRESS
New York

FIRST EDITION

All rights reserved, including the right of
reproduction in whole or in part in any form.

Copyright © 1995 by Jørgen Lyngbye, M.D., Ph.D.

Published by Vantage Press, Inc.
516 West 34th Street, New York, New York 10001

Manufactured in the United States of America
ISBN: 0-533-11247-8

Library of Congress Catalog Card No.: 94-90465

0 9 8 7 6 5 4 3 2 1

To Jintana

"This is an excellent idea; a concept of true sharing."
—Said about the Twin Concept by Sunitha Gandhi, Economist, The World Bank, at the UN Summit, Copenhagen, 1995.

Contents

Preface — ix
Introduction — xi
   The Amish — xii

1. The Background — 1
   Rich versus Poor — 1
2. Two Stories from Africa and One from Asia — 9
   A Scandinavian Family in Africa — 9
   The Views of a University Lecturer — 12
   A Success Story from Asia? — 15
3. Economy and the Poor — 17
4. The World Organizations — 28
   NAFTA — 28
   AFTA and APEC — 30
   The EU — 31
   GATT — 32
   OECD — 33
   Winners and Losers — 34
5. Religion and the Poor — 37
   A Global Ethic — 41
6. Be Twins — 43

Concluding Remarks — 51
Select References — 53

Preface

In the years 1970–75, I was member of a group led by a distinguished astronomer, Peter Naur. This was the first group in Scandinavia to work with world ecology and especially with problems of increasing world population and pollution. We at that time worked out models to cope with these problems, and it was felt rather as an academic task. Peter Naur is a most erudite mathematician, too, and it was really fun to work with him. But then it happened.

In 1978, people from three African nations came to my home city and told me about life in the countryside. This was an impressive experience. It was a story of hunger and utmost hardship. What before seemed a distant scenario in a dim future, now suddenly was just there—so close that you seemed to feel it with your own hands. Shortly after came Paul Harrison's classic *Inside the Third World—the Anatomy of Poverty,* a book you don't easily forget. These two events changed my outlook.

From that time on I didn't work out academic scenarios. I wanted to find solutions. The scenarios were already there. Every day human beings in Africa starved and died. We have since had reports again and again each year from the United Nations, the European Economic Community (EEC), and other powerful sources, but if you dig down under the surface of the words, nothing really has happened. I have my thoughts about the reasons for this, as you may have, too, and I shall come back to them later. So this is not just another book or report about the state of affairs. This is a result of work with the intention of finding a new course.

The idea of "twin countries" came about ten years ago and has since been discussed with many people, who have called upon me to write this book. The book is intended to be a simple one, easy for everyone to understand who has the faintest concern about the future of humanity. I know that this concept will be criticized. I certainly shall be attacked by politicians, officials, and experts. They will say that I am naive and that my concept it impossible because of the rules and regulations of the European Union (EU), NAFTA, GATT, and whatever. But we are talking about human systems only, where all that is wanted by the ones in power is possible. This is only a matter of choice. As Richard Feynman said, "Only basic physical laws like gravity can't be changed." Nothing more needs to be said.

Introduction

I had a good friend in Copenhagen, Denmark. He was a man of unusual integrity and intelligence, but he never got the influence or recognition that would come naturally to most people of his kind. He had the idea that "inebriation" with material products and the large multinational companies that produced these were the main obstacles to a true and honest human life. In its most grotesque and evil form it was the production of arms and the companies that made profit from this. He called it the black union of power.

He was an extremely talented writer, and he thought of letters as a sort of art. He decided to test out his philosophy in his own life. He thus lived as an ascetic in a couple of small rooms under the roof of an old building in the most modest part of the city, surrounded by papers, notes, and books. He calculated the interdependence of food nutritional value and price of production and thus the way to live cheaply on the best kind of nutrition and how humanity could avoid production of technology of useless and destructive kinds, especially arms.

In another place and century he would have been a highly respected man of wisdom, with many followers. But that isn't the way life is in a rich country of the late twentieth century. What counts to most is money, luxury, and a high lifestyle.

I lost sight of him ten years ago, but I kept all his letters.

The Amish

When you drive on the highway in Illinois you may come upon a sign that says: "Amish territory, 10 miles." A few miles later, further signs indicate that you have entered the territory. You see Amish shops with cheese and jam and maybe even an Amish guest house.

You can find the Amish several places in the United States, where they live close together in villages of their own.

This day, late autumn in a maize field in Illinois, you get sight of a younger man with a large beard, blue trousers with suspenders, white shirt, and black hat. He stands behind his horses at work with a tool. It is time for harvest. From your tour guide you already know that this man is married; he wears a beard.

Along the road you observe one maize field after another. In front of the small farmhouses you see carriages for transport of goods and passengers, and on the road you pass a black buggy with two passengers, one a middle-aged man in black with a hat and a white shirt. Behind him you can faintly see his wife. You have a feeling of another time fifty years ago.

The Amish people live like their forefathers, without use of the most common technical tools, without electricity, without telephones, and certainly without TV. They are farmers and make their living on the products of the soil. They are thrifty people, save their money, pay cash for property, and are self-sufficient with victuals. But some have problems because of declining prices on agricultural products, especially as they have to use horse power and avoid fertilizers.

In the village we meet a minister, who lives a close family life with his parents. Most Amish people don't want to mix, but he is an amiable man and allows you to see his house. And what do you find inside?

A young woman dressed in a long skirt and a white bonnet

works in the kitchen. It is his daughter, still unmarried. A living room with a few blue painted pieces of furniture made of wood by the minister himself and a couple of other rooms with only necessary tools. The Amish people are firm believers in God and distance themselves from all goods of materialism. "These values mean nothing to us. We base our lives on God, but it is important for us that each of us finds his own way to Him," relates the minister.

Within the family, the German language is spoken, even if more than 250 years have passed since the first Amish people came to the United States from Europe.

The roots of the Amish date back to sixteenth-century Switzerland, when they broke with the Catholic church. In the next century, the Amish founded their tradition, i.e., a pious family life as farmers in groups living close together. But their peace was brutally broken by persecutions, and they were tied to wheels and burnt, drowned, or tortured to death. They eventually had to flee to live in the mountains and later to the United States. At present, we find more than a hundred thousand Amish people in the United States.

I want to relate these accounts because in a not-so-far-distant future, virtues of this kind might be sought after. We should not be afraid of useful technology, but we have experienced a rapid rise in world population on our small globe with limited resources, which we all have to share.

TWINS

Chapter 1
The Background

The principal mechanisms by which the poor get poor: natural impoverishment, and ecological impoverishment; social impoverishment; the impoverishment of unequal exchange and of unequal competition.
—Paul Harrison, 1979

In the following I shall give a short sketch of the background, short because sufficient knowledge for action is already available. What is needed is the political will to seek ways to act and to understand how urgent the call for action has become. We have only a short time.

In what follows the POCs are defined as the twenty to thirty poorest countries of the world.

Rich versus Poor

A hundred years ago we were 1 billion people. This year we are 5.7 billion. In 2050, we will be at least 10 billion, maybe 12.

All people on our globe have the right to a fair life. Now, in 2050, and later.

These are not my words. They were stated by the United Nations in December 1948 in the well-known Declaration of Human Rights. From my point of view the most important article in the declaration is number 25.1: "Everyone has the right to a standard of living adequate for the health and well-being of himself and of his family, including food, clothing, housing and medical care and necessary social services, and the right to security in the event of unemployment, sickness, disability, widowhood, old age or other lack of livelihood in circumstances beyond his control." Please note the words: *food, housing, medical care,* and *lack of livelihood in circumstances beyond his control.*

Some of us were born in the United States, some in Bangladesh or Bolivia. This is beyond our control. But we all have the same rights to food and social security. Then what has happened in the last thirty years of "aid" to the poor countries? Really nothing. The rich got richer and the poor got poorer.

The new GATT agreement form, December 1993, has many intentions and nice words about an improved state of affairs, also for the poor. An improvement for each OECD citizen of thirty cents a day at a cost of one cent a day for the poorest in Africa.

They really have done something for article 25.1.

The theoretical presupposition for the assistance to the undeveloped POCs has been that they should be slowly raised to a welfare equal to that of the United States and Western Europe. This obviously is impossible because of the unacceptable costs for our environment, a fact that makes a new way of action urgent.

At present it looks like the political world managers ignore the major scenario of the next century. They keep busy with minor steps to improve this or that, but when it comes to the main task they seem in a paralyzed state. Why?

Because they don't know or dare to tell what to do. They have kept on telling the citizens of the rich world about improvements caused by their actions so as to be elected next time. They have said over and again that an increase in material welfare, explicitly money, is the only lifestyle that matters. Soon they shall have to eat their own words, because this scenario is impossible in the not-so-far-distant future. It may soon be too late or difficult to change people's attitudes toward money for more important immaterial values of life.

Under a surface of order and apparent rational actions, there is a state of perplexity. Those of us in the rich countries think that overconsumption and an overflow of more or less superfluous or useless products give a meaningful way of life, and we chose our political leaders accordingly. Their actions are predictable. But our globe is short of time and calls for changes in the traditional pattern of action. Just a few examples of what may happen.

There has come up a group of high-income international experts in economy who travel around the world and tell the poor countries what to do. These people are influential and have the power to let things happen for countries and even continents. They have often thought in macroprojects in the billion-dollar class, e.g., in cooperation with multinational companies. They discuss with local upper-class officials or big business, and the money is invested in a large factory, dam, or whatever. Or the money just disappears into the pockets of the local "fat cats." The family members of high-ranking government officials or politicians may be put in as managers, which, according to sources from the World Bank (WB) meeting, 1994, is just what is going to happen to aid from a Scandinavian to an African country.

All this happens, of course, under control of the foreign investors and government officials, who want employment for their people and profits for themselves. A meaningful use of less money based on knowledge about the countryside and local needs might have changed a whole region of the country concerned.

The International Monetary Fund (IMF) gave advice to Zimbabwe. Their advice was that the government should sell their stock of maize in order to pay the interest on their foreign debt. A short time after came the drought, and the stocks were badly needed. Some experts from Europe got support to establish a project in Zambesi. They hired expensive office localities and gave themselves high salaries. Some plans were made, but nothing more happened. I have been informed by a high-ranking UN official that this isn't the only occasion of that kind. Truly it certainly is not what takes place every time, but it reveals what can happen.

But how is life for ordinary people in the poor countries? Let us take a short look at two of the poorest, i.e., Bolivia in South America and Burkina Faso in Africa.

The Danish organization DanChurchAid reported on life in Bolivia. Ten percent of the children die before the age of ten, and more than half of the population doesn't have clean water. Bolivia is the poorest country in South America, and it is caught in a huge debt, which increases each year. The debt is now six times larger than the total yearly export, and new loans will follow if the country obeys the demand of the rich countries, i.e., privatizes its economy and keep tariffs at a low level. This means, among other things, free import of cheap dry milk from Europe, and the total result of these events will be destruction of the milk production of the poor farmers. DanChurchAid asks: "When shall we reduce the debt of the poor countries without at the same time demanding an economic policy that will make them even poorer?"

In Burkina Faso the average income is $290 per year, and the average life span is forty years. According to the United Nations, the illiteracy rate is 80 percent, and the share of industry in GNP is below 10 percent. No physicians are available in the countryside.

A Scandinavian country has declared that assistance has to be established in places only where it is expected to be lucrative for its own private companies. Support to the poor countries seems, thus, mainly meant to create more profit or jobs in the rich world. This means aid to relatively more prosperous countries like those of Southeast Asia and Venezuela, Chile, and Gabon in preference to the poor.

If poor countries are defined as places with a GNP of less than $1,800 per person per year, then apart from South Africa, only three countries in Africa are above this limit: Gabon, Botswana, and Libya.

Few people from the industrial or business sectors of rich societies want to support schools, health services, or other social improvements in the POCs south of the Sahara, or the ones in South America, for that matter. They want to deliver the goods produced at maximum profit, and there is no way to do so in the POCs. What we have often counts more than what they need. Furthermore, it is well known that the trade surplus in Japan and Germany in the eighties was invested to cover the budget deficit in the United States and not in the Third World.

We usually point out that overpopulation is a problem of the undeveloped countries. It is important to realize that overpopulation isn't a problem of the poor countries only. Overpopulation is not only a matter of counting people. For each person counted, one must include his consumption and his share in pollution. When you count this way, Western Europe and the United States are grossly overpopulated. Furthermore, dense population should not be mixed up with overpopulation. Dense population doesn't matter if the soil is fertile and intensive methods of cultivation are used. In places where this isn't the case, even a sparse population can't survive. It is a sad fact that the food production in Africa has decreased over the years and that the increase rate in Asia is small.

For a POC it is possible to multiply the food production if soil-preserving efforts and modern technology are used. Use of fertilizers is still low in the POCs south of the Sahara. There is a potential here, but it may be limited by the lack of water.

In addition, still unused areas for cultivation are available to a high degree where they are most needed, i.e., in Africa and in South America. In Asia, the possibilities for expansion are fewer, and the risk of severe harm to the environment and erosion is imminent.

New land for cultivation could be gained from deserts in Africa and Asia, where they cover vast areas, but at present these seem to be expanding. Aid from the rich world is urgently needed to overcome that problem. If so, lack of food will not be the main problem for the future. In the report "State of the World 1994," from the Worldwatch Institute, Lester Brown said that "achieving a humane balance between food and people now depends more on family planning than on farmers." He sees as the main problem the growing imbalance between food and people and the solution to be increasing international efforts in family planning.

Family planning is important, but his views on food production are self-contradictory. First he points out that the production of grain doesn't increase because the resources are limited, and later he states that the reason is a decreasing demand because of a drop in income in the undeveloped world.

I don't agree with his views. There is a vast potential for production of the two major crops in the world, i.e., wheat and rice: wheat, for example, in Russia and Eastern Europe and rice in Asia. This was convincingly shown in recent reports by John Bongaarts and Peter T. White. John Bongaarts concludes that feeding a growing world population a diet that improves over time in quality and quantity is technologically feasible, but the economic and environmental costs may well prove too great for many poor countries. I agree with Mr. Bongaarts. The main problem will turn out to be poverty, especially in the POCs.

Peter T. White points out that more than 90 percent of the world's rice is produced in Asia, with about 60 percent in China and India alone. Most of the rice production is consumed locally. Chief exporters of rice are Thailand, the United States and

Vietnam, but only 4 percent of world production is traded. The world production of rice is less than half of the total production of wheat and corn, but 20 percent of wheat and as much as 65 percent of corn went to feed livestock, so rice is the world's number-one food crop for humans. Furthermore, the rice plant is so adaptable that it is fully possible to "redesign" it to produce a greater yield. It should also be noted that the low prices on grain products during the eighties resulted in a decreased use of fertile soil during that period.

In addition, the UN Food and Agriculture Organization (FAO), in October 1993, said that many valuable food crops rich in protein and oil, apart from the well-known wheat, rice, maize, and potatoes, are possible as future food sources, e.g., *tarwi* and *olluca* from South America and the *marama* bean from Africa. Furthermore, it is possible, with a more intensive use of gene technology, to develop valuable new plant products also for human consumption.

But the vast waste of food energy and the erosion of environment caused by breeding of cattle should certainly also be mentioned in this context. All in all, there is a large reserve capacity for food production.

New land for cultivation should certainly not be gained from the forests. The cutting down of forest for timber and gain of land is disastrous, and unfortunately, some of the richest countries, like, e.g., Japan, have imported large amounts of timber. In Southeast Asia, for example, the rain forest was 50 percent of the total area around the Second World War but has now, unfortunately, shrunk to 10 percent.

With a fast increase in population, the lack of access to clean, fresh water is often a most serious obstacle. Water polluted by contagious material is a disaster to a POC. On the other hand, water plants have been built on false premises in several places for use in large industrial constructions. Such water plants have caused loss of fertile soil and clean water in both India and Pakistan.

The UN meeting on the world environment in Rio in 1992 was a disappointment. The UN world environment plan, "Agenda 21," did not get the necessary economic support, and a promise from all developed countries to give 0.7 percent of the GNP as aid to the poor before the year 2000 was not given in a credible way.

Chapter 2
Two Stories from Africa and One from Asia

Go out quickly into the streets and lanes of the city, and bring in here the poor and the maimed and the lame and the blind.
—Luke 14:21

Africa might be the continent that suffers most from poverty, hunger, and, unfortunately, political unrest and wars, too. According to UNDP's Human Development Report 1993, nine of the ten poorest countries in the world were African. The tenth was Afghanistan.

Two recent "stories" from Africa might therefore be of interest, published in a book and as a newspaper column, respectively. They are statements on present-day Africa. Though they are not related, they give an impression of the situation right now.

The third story is from Asia. Maybe a success?

A Scandinavian Family in Africa

Africa is hunger, AIDS, and war. Many die every day and the number is broadcast for us to keep in mind that we must take these problems seriously. But do we still listen when we wash up in our kitchen or drink our coffee? It is so far away and you can really do nothing.

But the remote events come to life when suddenly a Danish family placed in the middle of African reality gives their report on return: barbed wire in South Africa, land mines in Angola, bankruptcy in Zaire, AIDS in Uganda, drought in Ethiopia, skeletons on a beach in Eritrea, and Islamic dictatorship in Sudan. Who would believe that it could be possible to follow this route of death and devastation? Anyhow, this was what Hjalte and Nina Rasmussen have done together with their grown-up children Emil and Ida. Emil can now drive his own bike, and as for fair-haired Ida, her father had a lucky day when he was offered ten thousand camels for her, as he was told that she could be a sharp—and lovely—wife.

This tour from Cape to Cairo is trip number four for the family and the hardest one, too, as told by Hjalte.

In spite of the harsh circumstances, Africa isn't just misery. This family meets wonderful untouched scenery and persons able to produce every tool they need and, above all, a kindness and hospitality that seem completely forgotten in Western countries.

The Africans live fully in daily life, and love feasts and colors even under the worst imaginable conditions. This kind of life implies that it is difficult for people to use Western aid in the way it is given. Everywhere Hjalte and Nina are met by signs of poverty and decay. In larger cities garbage and wrecked cars are seen and the buildings are not kept in repair. The huts of common Africans are in a poor condition.

It is thinkable that the present Western aid doesn't help the Africans in the long run. It might even spoil more than it benefits, because it isn't at all adapted to the need of the receivers. People who live on assistance forget to raise cattle, and some who are lucky enough to get soy oil might use the plastic can to bring home liquor.

The soft spot in emergency aid is, callously spoken; Why keep people alive when a large problem of Africa is overpopulation? What will happen in Ethiopia when the population has grown so rapidly that it is impossible to feed its people even in years without drought? Nina feels sure that unless you really improve the standard of living for people and thus reduce the number of births, makeshift food and medicine will only result in even poorer conditions in this continent of suffering.

But also the more far-seeing aid has its weak spots under the present conditions.

In Kenya the family meets an experienced aid worker, who relates how difficult it can be to find use for foreign aid: "It isn't easy at all; this year I have $30 million, but I can't think of enough projects to use all that money!"

As for Hjalte and Nina, it looks like the present administration of foreign aid has become the vat of the Danaides. Maybe this type of aid is running more for the sake of the Western organizations than for the Africans. Furthermore, some of the money may end up in the pockets of rich Africans because of corruption.

"If you look here and there you can find minor progress such as, for example, a new school, cleaner water in a village or a health center, so that fewer babies die or some new trees are planted. But the present aid will leave an Africa even more overpopulated and poor. The truth is that Africa by any means has become poorer in the last thirty years," Hjalte writes.

They came to admire many common Africans for their humanity and strength in enduring the hard terms of life. There seem to exist human resources in Africa, but the current type and management of Western aid is a failure.

The Views of a University Lecturer

George B. N. Ayittey, a lecturer at the American University in Washington, D.C., is critical of the aid, too. I want to quote him because he represents another and a more traditional "expert" kind of view, which places the responsibility for the problems on the Africans themselves. He relates that Africa is rich in resources and raw materials but holds the view that the Africans, or rather the African governments have spoiled the opportunities. As for raw materials, Africa's part of the world total is 90 percent of cobalt, 64 percent of manganese, 50 percent of phosphate, 40 percent of platinum, the main part of diamonds, and a potential of 40 percent of world hydroelectric power.

The mineral production of Africa is of significance in several industries, such as steel, oil, gold, platinum, atomic power, and space flight. But Ayittey means that incompetence in leadership has spoiled the opportunities and caused poverty. Many governments nationalized foreign property and mining and condemned free competition, free markets, and democracy. In Tanzania and Guinea, traditional trade was doomed, and in Ghana, markets were burned. In Zaire, President Mobuto expropriated foreign property and expelled Belgian business people, plantation owners, technical staffs, etc. According to Mr. Ayittey, Mobuto then gave it all to his friends and to members of his tribe, with the result that all profit disappeared from Zaire; in 1988 a sum of $400 million from export shall not have been accounted for.

In Togo the phosphate mines were nationalized in the seventies and their income was confiscated by presidents. Also in the seventies, in Nigeria, a state-owned oil company took control of the oil industry. Here the average income per capita is lower than at independence in 1960.

Mr. Ayittey means that economic systems successful in other parts of the world don't work in Africa. In East Asia and in Chile these systems have succeeded in spite of dictatorship, corruption, and violation of human rights, which were "tolerated" if the dictator certified stability and "correct" economy. African dictators have "spoiled" one economy after the other, and thus the Africans demand democracy to get rid of incompetent regimes. The intention of reformation of society is inconsiderable, and reforms are only implemented in order to stabilize ruling governments or to gain control over the economy.

According to Mr. Ayittey, foreign interests should spend no effort on reformation of regimes but rather take interest in the activities of society of interest for the population such as subdue inflation rates, establish an independent banking system, and implement taxes on income, consumption, and business activities.

Mr. Ayittey relates that after the collapse of Soviet communism in 1991 continuation of foreign aid to several countries, e.g., Malawi and Kenya, has been made conditional on implementation of democracy. A consequence of this was establishment of a sort of democracy with several parties in these countries, but the opposition gained only minor access to mass media, the judges were pro-government, and rules and regulations were introduced to secure the power of rulers.

Ayittey states that stable market reforms can't survive unless independent courts are introduced, confiscation of private property and companies is stopped, and the governments are prevented from manipulation of currency. The foreign aid organizations should pay no attention to the charisma of dictators but, rather, let the Africans fight for reformation.

The secretary-general of the All African Church Council (AACC), Mr. José Chipenda, makes significant comments on the situation that are relevant to the beliefs of Mr. Ayittey. Mr. Chipenda is a modern African observer of great knowledge and integrity, himself being a citizen of Angola. "Democracy isn't the same as a multi-party system. When the West demands democratization in Africa they refer to a model that isn't suited for us.

Democracy is the ability to adapt to changes and novel situations. It is certainly not the same as to have a register of seventy parties for election as you can see in Cameroon," states Mr. Chipenda. For example, Zambia and Kenya have been forced to introduce a multiparty "democracy," but that certainly doesn't transform these countries into "democratic" nations. Great Britain has only three parties and just two large ones. Seen from outside, these are rather identical in policy.

So far there may be some agreement between Mr. Ayittey and Mr. Chipenda. But further on Mr. Chipenda states that imposition of this "democracy" is an inappropriate neo-colonialistic mark in a process of reformation. During the cold war the West showed an immense interest in selling arms to Africa in support of various dictatorships, but no one spoke of "democracy." "The cold war kept many dictators alive," killed many Africans and ruined elementary human rights for even more, relates Mr. Chipenda. This behavior has created much damage in Africa, and now we suddenly see this change to a kind of double morality, "business as usual." As for Angola, the Great Powers meant that it was "smart" to get oil and gold by use of military aid. At present nobody in the West talks about arms. No apology and only insignificant support are given to those who suffer because the way to true democracy was crippled by those actions. This applies to Angola but certainly we have completely analogous situations in many countries of our continent.

José Chipenda sees the AACC as a crucial instrument in the process of democratization and implementation of true human rights, and a center of knowledge in the transformation ahead. He has taken part in negotiations between the resistance and leaders in many places on the African continent.

A Success Story from Asia?

Is Vietnam to be the new "adventure" of Southeast Asia? After the end of the Vietnam War in 1975, Vietnam was isolated internationally in spite of some aid from the Soviet Union. In 1986 the Communist party decided to give up Marxism and allow foreign investment in cooperation with other countries of Southeast Asia.

In the last seven years there has been rapid change in Vietnam. Vietnam is still one of the poorest countries in the world, but with one of the highest growth rates. The country has a population of 70 million, a surplus of raw materials, and a disciplined and relatively well educated work force and, on average, one of the lowest salary levels in Asia.

Vietnam seems to have followed Taiwan, Singapore, and South Korea, and some believe that the country fifty years from now will reach a standard of living close to that of Western Europe. So you could guess that Vietnam wants to improve welfare before "closing time," i.e., enter the club of rich countries before the world resource crisis sets in sometime in the next century.

A factor of some importance may be that President Clinton in 1994 lifted the embargo against Vietnam, but the countries in East Asia have been the first ones to place investments in the new partner.

The government in Hanoi started to gradually introduce market reforms in 1987, and this took place almost without aid from the outside except for some consultations with the United Nations. In 1988 the inflation rate in Vietnam was 1,000 percent, the export nearly 0, and food production low. Vietnam has voluntarily introduced the reforms recommended by the World Bank (WB) and International Monetary Fund (IMF). A strict financial policy has resulted in a decrease in the inflation rate to 4 percent; many concerns owned by the state have been closed and workers transferred to private business. The growth rate is now 8 percent and the export of, for example, rice has shown a marked increase. With an investment of $40 billion in the next years it might be possible to double the GNP. In 1993 Vietnam was promised in the first place a sum of $1.7 billion from the Western world in order to reinforce the infrastructure.

The legal system is insufficient and corruption is present to a certain degree.

Many people in Vietnam are dissatisfied with the cuts in industry, which have resulted in unemployment, and furthermore, much of the free service in education and medical care has been removed.

The sad followers of liberalism, social inequality and beggars show up in the cities. Vietnam is still a dictatorship and it is interesting, as mentioned elsewhere, that none of the "successful" countries in this part of Asia have been democracies by the Western meaning of the word. The government has been authoritarian in all of them. It should be remembered that the condition set by the Western countries for further aid to Africa is implementation of "Democracy," and this is probably not only because of the protection of human rights.

The "success" in Southeast Asia has been a result of strict governmental management, with little or no influence from the community. A well-known Vietnamese scientist says that Vietnam today shows a contradiction between the wish of the Communist party to preserve power and dictatorship and forces of the free market.

I feel that the considerations in these stories touch different aspects of the economies, or you could even say fates, of the undeveloped countries and they could thus be an introduction to the next chapter.

Chapter 3
Economy and the Poor

Ah, happily do we live, greedless among the greedy;
Amidst greedy men, greed-free we dwell.
—Dhammapada, vv. 197–200

The first and most important fact is that economic systems are created by human beings. This implies that they can and must be changed by humans. The so-called laws of economy are certainly not untouchable, like the laws of physics—an impression you may have if you listen to experts in economics. Several years of study have convinced me that a not-insignificant number of these laws were created with a mirror to the past and that revision is needed. It seems like only a few of these experts understand the need and nature of the revision necessary, so the initiative and first steps have to come from outside.

For the first time in history we have reached a point where experience is of little use, because the present and, even more, the future situation will be unique for mankind. To neutralize outdated views is often the hardest job, because so much prestige and power has been invested. From my contacts with experts I have the feeling that their traditional belief is an obstacle to achieving valid solutions to control poverty. This may imply a novel basis for economics and the rejection of beliefs that might cause damage and delay necessary actions. This basis must be created by many people with the most varied backgrounds. Unfortunately, we are in a situation where experts in economics have a unique influence on political decisions on a worldwide basis, so the task turns out to be a hard one. Their views are for the same reason "universally acknowledged" and therefore extremely difficult to challenge. Wrong decisions can easily be the result. In a not-so-distant future this fact may be fatal to many people around the world.

The purpose of economic systems is production for consumption, that is, transformation of the resources of nature to goods and services through the use of investment and labor. These goods may be useful, useless, or even harmful (e.g., arms), but in principle the economic system and laws do not "care" what kind of goods are produced or the costs to the environment.

Some experts have the view, though, that these costs have to be reflected in the price of goods. But this isn't enough; a radical change in economic models is necessary. Several natural resources are already at present extremely limited, and furthermore, the capacity for deposit of waste products in soil, sea, and air decreases each year. This of course also applies to useless and harmful goods, which, regrettably, are profitable and therefore make up a considerable part of world production.

In the last forty years the richer nations have earned more than 80 percent of world income and in the same time span been responsible for 80 percent of the carbon dioxide pollution. In the OECD countries the energy consumption is ten times larger than in South America, twenty times larger than in India, and fifty times larger than in the poorest part of Africa. In 1960, when the foreign aid to the POCs began, the income in the developed countries was about thirty times higher. In 1990, after thirty years of aid, the gap had doubled to sixty times in the POCs' disfavor. So that is what the success of the foreign "aid" looks like.

A widely held view among economic experts is that the developed countries must have economic growth to create a basis for growth in the Third World. This view is dangerous and may lead to a serious world situation, as it is held by some powerful political leaders, too. A 3–4 percent increase rate in income in the United States until the year 2004 will give a rise in the average per capita income of seven to eight thousand dollars over this ten-year period. In the POCs in Africa the same figure is calculated at forty to fifty dollars, that is, 100–200 times less at best.

The interdependence between increase in population and economic growth is complicated. An increased demand for health service, education, and infrastructure is evident, but on the other side there are more people to pay the costs. Again the POCs are the losers because of low technology and savings. The high birthrate is certainly coupled with the social insecurity that results from poverty.

It is important to control population growth, which at present is 3–4 percent yearly in the African POCs south of the Sahara and in some parts of South Asia, i.e., on the average seven children per adult female.

This is especially evident when the capital for the necessary minimum investments in education, health service, and agriculture are not available, as is the case in the POCs in Africa and South Asia. Therefore, the main factor in population control is increase in welfare in the poorest countries. When the increase in population is high and the increase in new jobs is slow, lower salaries are a sure consequence.

The undeveloped countries' part of total world trade increased from 20 percent in 1970 to 30 percent in 1988, but only one-quarter of products from POCs in Africa were industrialized goods. In addition, prices on raw materials and food products are sensitive to demand on the world market, e.g., in OECD, where heavy-handed trade regulations hurting the POCs were introduced in 1987–89. This caused a loss in income for the POCs equal to the official aid in the same period. This proved especially harmful to their exporting of industrialized goods. In the poor countries there are still large resources of some raw materials but no capital or know-how for production. As a consequence the POCs are tempted to sell out raw materials at low prices in order to buy consumer goods and technology. This is a dangerous tendency and must be avoided; furthermore, an increase in debt is a sure consequence of this policy.

I have a feeling that decisive factors for the economic and environmental conditions are the sparse and ineffective foreign aid, perhaps combined with incompetent local political management, rather than the religious beliefs, local cultural traditions, or maybe even the population growth rate. One important factor is the high costs in an ineffective industry caused by lack of capital, coordination, and know-how. Others are ineffective cultivation methods in farming and, especially in Africa, lack of capital for cultivation of large as-yet-unused areas.

The prospect for these countries is gloomy as far as their own ability to mobilize resources and investments for improvement of welfare and environmental conditions through better technology. Their only hope for a future is a novel major initiative from the rich world, which is a radical break with the policy conducted up to now. This means a stop to a little help here and there to this and that and starting up anew. Willingness to cover the real costs and to cut off the surplus of consumption in the richest countries of the world is the number-one demand.

The challenge is enormous and in this book it is only possible to sketch it briefly.

The first step is development of a basis designed to gradually unite two or more initially different economies in a closely knit system of equal partners. By this I don't mean a unity like we see in the EU between rich countries, but a union of a continuum of industrialized and agrarian systems. A new type of management mechanism must be developed, as an unmodified market management system will prove inadequate in this kind of economy. Exact and detailed information has to form the basis for formulation of such a strict management system as shall function in the period of knitted economies.

This system must be suited for the unification from a starting position of a poor agricultural system with low consumption and a rich industrialized system with overconsumption. How shall the internal economy be coordinated and how shall internal and external export be integrated in this structure? How can two economies work together for equal access to effective technology? How can we use price policy in order to yield conditions for poor farmers to, at the same time, cultivate the soil effectively and care for the environment? How can we press the United States and the EU to remit debt as improvement progresses?

With this, action is necessary, not talk. The view of Susan George on the deadly debt is still true. An effective and flexible working between public output and performance and the market coordinated with a stable political system is important for the operation of the involved societies in a fair and effective way as well as for confidence in the legal, social, and economic system.

It is necessary, with a gradual resource reduction in the high consumption partner, for a partnership to create common social justice and welfare for the whole system. This may prove to be a most difficult part of the process but can be helped by establishment of cooperative ownership systems. I shall elaborate on this topic in chapter 6.

In the *World Science Report* of 1994 from UNESCO it is said that more than 80 percent of scientific research takes place in the richest countries, i.e., the United States, EU and Japan.

UNESCO shows great admiration for the rapid development in certain Asian countries such as, for example, South Korea, Taiwan, and Singapore. In South Korea the GNP has grown from around $2 to $169 billion in the period 1962–1988. It is stressed that this has only been possible because the science and technology policy has been based on the demands of the world market.

But this and other expert reports have indicated that poverty and famine can be prevented in the future if the Asian model is copied by the POCs in South America and Africa.

I feel that this worldview is naive. Education and relevant technology will of course benefit South America and Africa, too, but why did East Asia prosper? The answer is that they came first. They were the first to develop high-tech (e.g., luxury) products that could be sold to the United States and Europe.

If we for a moment imagine that all countries in South America and Africa simultaneously had done the same as, for example, South Korea, then the world would indeed have been brought to a difficult situation. The world resources would have been exhausted and impoverished, with partly useless consumption of energy and raw materials. As mentioned, such an increase in the state of living would not be possible without a major reduction of the overconsumption in Europe and North America.

The policies of the WB and the IMF have up to now been prescribing strictly free-market solutions such as liberalization and privatization to help nations develop. From the eighties the WB has imposed harsh demands of devaluation and reduction of the public sector in order to create growth in, e.g., Africa. In the same period loans with a high interest rate from IMF have ruined the possibility of new investment.

The views of the WB have often been one-sided, but an official has told me that the WB feels guilt-free concerning the crisis of the POCs, which according to WB officials started before any initiative was taken by them. In 1989, WB policy was criticized by UNICEF for lack of human dimension. The WB seems now to have improved a few programs for health and education, but to a small effect when seen in connection with the loan policy of the IMF. They have proscribed the notion of picking winners, e.g., South Korea and, obviously, Japan in the marketplace but have had to concede that state-managed growth and authoritarian rule have been central in the process. As mentioned above they have thought of these nations as models for the rest of the poor world.

In the 1994 report *World Economic Outlook* from IMF there seems to be some improvement in understanding compared to what we have seen earlier from their economic experts, and I shall therefore refer to this report in some detail. For the undeveloped countries as a group the standard of living has improved in later years. The increase in production has on the average been 6 percent yearly, i.e., substantially more than in the United States and EU. In 1994 and 1995 the figures are expected to be 5.5 and 5.8 percent, respectively.

But these figures gloss over large differences between the different undeveloped countries. In Southeast Asia the economic growth rate has been up to 8 percent and in China even 13 percent in 1992 and 1993. The same level is expected for 1994. In India increasing growth in 1993 reached 4 percent. Only Burma and the Philippines are lagging behind. At present the standard of living in Singapore, Taiwan, South Korea, and Hong Kong is comparable to that in, say, Spain or Greece, and the level of education is high. The losers among continents are South America and especially Africa, but some countries on these continents, e.g., Argentina, Chile, Sudan, and Tunis, have a higher growth rate than the rest.

A main problem is, as before, the enormous debt. In Africa the growth rate was on average 0.4 percent in 1992 and about 1 percent in 1993. As for the poorest African countries, the growth rate could just outbalance the growth in population and the sad fact is that several of these have a lower standard of living than thirty years ago.

The IMF has its views on the reason(s) for the problems of the poorest countries. Accordingly, it should be a complex of insufficient administration, wrong policy, lack of incitement to reform society, and, in addition, an unfavorable international influence on economy.

The countries with the highest savings rate have the opportunity to invest in future production and thus improve their situation. But how can you save or invest when you have a sky-high debt and a rapidly growing population to feed? I feel there might be an increase in understanding the importance of remittal of debt and not, like before, when some were advised to sell food reserves to pay the interest. According to the IMF, the situation of the French-speaking African countries is somewhat better because of devaluation of their currency (CFA franc) and here a growth rate is expected to increase to maybe 4 percent.

But a most depressing fact is that the successful countries are probably the ones that will succeed even more in the future. Populations larger than the ones in the United States and Europe will here press forward and upward to a standard of living and, in a not-so-far distant future, to an overconsumption like ours. Foreign investors and multinational companies will be attracted for profit. Luxury or even useless goods will have an increasing share of the total production. The environment shall suffer, erosion and pollution increase, and the poor in our world will be pressed down and become even poorer. Unrest, invasion of richer regions, and even war may result, because no one tolerates an inequality of this dimension in the long run.

In 1992–93 some new thoughts on the future were published. Donella H. and D. L. Meadows and J. Randers calculated that the world economy has to increase by a factor of twenty-one if it is to sustain a population of, say, 12.5 billion at the same standard of living as in the United States today. We thus would have to find twenty industrial worlds in addition to the one we have now. If we wanted to keep the environmental problems on the same level as today, we in the rich world would have to reduce use of resources and the level of pollution per capita to 5 percent of the level that we have today. The authors recommend a drastic reduction in use of resources, growth of population, and world capital.

To curb poverty a major transfer from the rich to the poor sectors of the world will be necessary, and if so, all can use enough resources, but the difficulty is to agree upon what "enough" means. The authors seem to doubt that this development is possible in our democratic system with use of market economy as the tool. We must search for a novel system to overcome these difficulties.

Trygve Haavelsmo and Stein Hansen have similar concerns. They doubt the conclusions of the WCED report *Our Common Future* (1987), i.e., that it is possible to bring the poor countries up to the level of the industrialized world with the same pattern of consumption and investment as the rich countries. They mean that exhaustion of resources will result, so these goals are incompatible. According to the *World Bank Atlas 1991,* the GNP per capita on a world basis averaged to around four thousand dollars, but the same figure in a developed country (Norway) was twenty-three thousand dollars. So with equal share a reduction in the Norway standard of living of 80 percent is necessary. To attain this goal an internationally recognized organization must have the authority to set the course and the power to enforce the necessary action.

In Paul Kennedy's well-known book *Preparing for the Twenty-first Century,* we find an excellent analysis of world problems, but few solutions. He recommends that we should look for international leadership and give up our ties to the national state. According to Kennedy, education, especially of women, is important in order to subdue the rise in world population.

De we need a "motor" in economy? It has never been possible for me to understand the basis for the "motor" theory of economy. In the report *Our Common Future* this "motor" apprehension seems to be an assumption for the concept that growth in the rich world is necessary to establish growth in the Third World. But what have we seen recently?

In China and Southeast Asia there has been a rise in growth far steeper than in, e.g., the EU. This development has been nearly independent of ours, as these countries have had inner "motors" and have certainly not been "drawn" by the Western world. So it seems that the statements in the report are wrong, a view supported by Trygve Haavelsmo and Stein Hansen.

The right conclusion may be that growth in the rich world can cause neither growth in the Third World nor a major decline in unemployment in the EU or elsewhere. What is needed in the long run is a condition of balance based on a fair share of available work, establishment of new kinds of social employment, and a decrease in consumption, use of energy and pollution.

In addition I want to refer to a newly published book (1994) by Jeffrey Sachs: *Poland's Jump to the Market Economy*. Mr. Sachs has been an adviser to the government in Poland and, with less success, to the government in Russia, too. His views are thus of interest as an exponent for experts in economy of the late twentieth century.

From 1990 the economic system in Poland has gone through a radical change to liberalization and capitalism. The inflation rate has declined, over half of the GNP is now related to the private sector of society, and a part of the foreign debt has been eliminated. In spite of a difficult political situation in Poland, Sachs wants the Polish experiment to be copied by even more countries in Eastern Europe. He states that the changes will be a success if these countries twenty years from now have reached a standard of living close enough to Western standards to enter the EU. We find in Mr. Sachs's book only sparse considerations on the future consequences of this process for Africa and South America. Furthermore, he shares the common view of experts that the condition for close cooperation among countries is based on an equal level of wealth among parties.

Democracy in the individual countries is highlighted and, as related above, a kind of "democracy" with many parties has been forced upon some African nations as a condition for further aid. But we have no democracy on a world basis to manage what benefits the world population and the world environment as a whole. What happens is a sum of steps taken at random in relation to totality. Democracy or not, each country is sitting in its small cave and the contact, trade, etc., with other countries serves mainly individual interests. Management is difficult, so what is done is little, late, and left-handed. The United Nations has no real power, and pessimism spreads in the corridors, I was told by a high-ranking UN official.

Liberalism lost the battle in a too late moment of victory over communism, and future economic growth in the traditional sense of this conception is certainly an illusion of our time. In order to maintain the idea of richness and a high standard of living, which the whole world obviously can't obtain because of the limited resources in a fast-growing population, we stick to that illusion. We seem to think that goods could conveniently be produced by the highly industrialized countries in Asia, e.g., Japan, Taiwan, and South Korea. We then offer to these countries and other richer ones our services, goods, and know-how so we can buy even more of their products, etc., etc. We dump the poorest. The illusion is then both complete and fulfilled.

Chapter 4
The World Organizations

It's not the debtor who decides when a default will occur—it's the lender.
—Susan George, 1988

In the following I shall try to shortly relate a few relevant facts on the three main trade organizations, NAFTA, AFTA, and EU, and, in addition, on APEC, GATT, and OECD. It is certainly not my intention to give a complete overview; that is obviously not possible within this frame or even relevant for our present purpose. On the other hand, it is impossible to ignore the rules and regulations agreed upon and the future consequences for the POCs.

NAFTA

As is well known, NAFTA stands for the North American Free Trade Agreement. It took power in January 1994 and eliminated tariffs and other trade barriers among the United States, Canada, and Mexico, covering 360 million people. Tariffs will be eliminated over a period of fifteen years, with more than 60 percent elimination over the first five years. Levies on forty-five hundred products were phased out immediately. Mexican tariffs on U.S. products averaged about 10 percent and U.S. tariffs on Mexican products about 4 percent. As for finance, Mexico shall allow Canadian and U.S. banks, insurance companies, and brokers free access after a period of some years during which bans on foreign ownership shall be phased out. Mexico can avoid high duty on shipment of textiles to Canada and the United States as long as clothing is made from fabrics and yarn from North America.

As for farming, tariffs are eliminated on most products. On sensitive products a period of several years is allowed for adjustment; for example, for the United States asparagus, melons, concentrate of orange juice and sugar and for Mexico dry beans and corn. The import licenses of Mexico shall be phased out; these used to cover 25 percent of the U.S. exports.

With respect to technology Mexico shall allow foreigners to invest in trucking companies. Trucking companies in the whole region shall be allowed to do business even on international roads prohibited before. After some years, the North American content of auto cars shall increase from 50 to more than 60 percent, this to qualify for duty-free treatment.

In telecommunications, U.S. firms shall be allowed to compete for contracts from the Public Telephone System of Mexico and investment restrictions will be eliminated.

Commissions will be established to oversee laws of labor and environment. Sanctions shall be possible, e.g., fines or implementation of trade tariffs.

NAFTA is marked by the kind of fast-growth philosophy that is precarious, because it will stimulate unselective production and trade of large proportions, which is ecologically inappropriate just a few decades into the twenty-first century.

Obviously Mexico is the poorest country in NAFTA and it was not unexpected for experienced spectators that the suppressed population in southern Mexico rose against NAFTA and the government. Many were killed. In this part of Mexico rich landowners have all the power, and the social gap will grow with the future development.

NAFTA may expand in coming years; Argentina and other South American countries knock on the door.

AFTA and APEC

As you may know, AFTA stand for ASEAN Free Trade Area and is an organization of countries in Southeast Asia to establish a region of free trade. These countries recently agreed to reduce tariffs on about thirty thousand categories of goods.

On the other hand is the Asia-Pacific Economic Cooperation, or APEC, a consultative organization of eighteen countries, including the United States, Canada, Australia, New Zealand, Chile (from 1994), Japan, China, and some others in Southeast Asia.

The aim of APEC (and GATT) seems to contradict the purpose of NAFTA and AFTA, which is to establish free trade between a limited number of nations. There is considerable resistance against alteration of APEC to anything more than a loose structure. For example, China does not want any sort of community. But even in this case some reductions in tariffs were decided upon in 1993. A driving force is obviously the interest of the United States in a market of this size as the U.S. trade deficit in this area is about $90 billion. Just 1–2 percent share of this market would mean half a million new jobs in the United States, as the growth rate in the region by traditional calculation is estimated to average up to 7 percent per year.

In total, APEC comprises 60 percent of the world economy and 40 percent of total world trade, so if a firmer structure is established later, APEC certainly will be a force to reckon with. It is at present difficult to know what way APEC will go. If it is to become a new form of NAFTA or even amalgamated with NAFTA, we are confronted with a challenge of immense dimensions, affecting half of the world population. I personally am deeply concerned by this scenario and its consequences for world resources and environment.

The EU

Since November 1993 the former EEC was transformed to the European Union with the intention to establish closer ties between economies of the countries of Europe. I shall just briefly point out some tendencies of interest lately. Some of these were revealed in a report from the EU Commission in December 1993 and were no surprise, as they consisted of short-term actions for curbing unemployment, which has passed 10 percent and thus includes 15–20 million people, and more long-term changes in the economic and political union of Europe. Furthermore, education should be strengthened and infrastructure improved.

The means for curbing unemployment are of course the traditional ones, in the first place efforts to further increase growth in economy, but the competition with Asia and Eastern Europe makes this difficult. Some experts maintain that development of products of high technology combined with lower salaries and taxes on damage to environment and on pollution are necessary.

In the Maastricht treaty it is emphasized that the EU nations must intend "common actions" with a coordinated policy in foreign affairs, economy, and defense. In addition there is the expansion of the EU with the EFTA countries, i.e., Austria, Sweden, and Finland.

As for agriculture, the rich countries like the EU and also the United States use billions of dollars to stimulate their own farmers to overproduction and at the same time large sums to dump surplus on the world market and to contribute food to alleviate famine in the Third World. But famine is not always caused by drought and other kinds of disaster. Even under normal conditions, the trade and agriculture policy of the rich world (e.g., the EU) is an obstacle to the production of food products in the Third World, which of course is unacceptable. The reason for these actions of the rich world can only be fear of decrease in profit and rise in unemployment.

GATT

GATT, or the General Agreement on Trade and Tariffs, was established in 1947 and has as its members 117 countries, so this is now a power of large dimensions. The purpose of the agreement is to establish game rules for world trade.

As for the relation between the POCs and the rich world, the goals and effects of GATT are extremely important. GATT aims at an increase of world production of merchandise for a rise in the lifestyle of everyone, even those who are already rich at present. The philosophy is that trade should be nondiscriminatory, but this is certainly not without exceptions.

Since 1947 there have been eight steps in the progress of GATT, including the last one, valid since January 1994, and according to economic expertise a yearly growth in world economy of $200 billion will be the result. The main new aspects this time are the inclusion of agriculture as a total sector of economy and, further, of international investments and service output. Before, GATT covered only ordinary goods, but the new agreement includes services of banks, insurance companies, telecommunication, and international transport and communication; intellectual property like rights of patent and origin; international investment; and agriculture.

One of the main obstacles to the agreement was the U.S. demand for a cut in the EU support of the export of farming products. Thus EU must during a six-year period cut the amount of products given support by 21 percent.

The protection of intellectual property in all countries is an especially crucial advance to the industrialized nations and makes it possible to collect royalties worldwide. Investment in another country, e.g., establishment of factories or firms, is now subject to regulations so that, for example, it isn't necessary to buy equipment in that country only. Tariffs are on the average cut by one-third, and the multifiber agreement that used to protect the production of textiles in the industrialized nations will be phased out over a period of ten years. Shipping is in principle covered by the GATT agreement, but only to a minor effect. The aircraft industry was agreed upon by the United States and EU already in 1992. This limits the national support of the research and development of airplanes carrying more than one hundred passengers. This is expected to benefit the aircraft industry in the United States in competition with the European Airbus Company.

In January 1995 GATT will be replaced by an even more comprehensive organization, the World Trade Organization, which is able to react even faster to disagreements over trade among member nations.

The WB and OECD experts on economics estimate that the result of implementation of GATT will be an increase in growth of 1 percent worldwide, which will effect a reduction in unemployment and a fall in the prices of many goods. An alarming increase in consumption in the United States and EU can certainly be expected. This will damage the POCs initially, and later we shall certainly all pay the price.

OECD

OECD, the exclusive Organization for Economic Cooperation and Development in the industrialized world, was established in 1960 and has twenty-five members. The latest one,

Mexico, entered the organization in May 1994, and this is the first new member since 1973. The OECD has some prestige because it is a club of richer and more developed nations that gives advice and analyzes the economic situation of the world, but its importance to the POCs is more limited. However, the harmful trade regulations from the late eighties should not be forgotten, cf. chapter 3.

Winners and Losers

Who are the winners and losers in the big game of world trade? According to traditional economic theory, it is possible for two nations to both benefit from mutual trade, if they specialize their production, even if they are different in cost level and productive capacity. For example, a developed country specializing in high technology and a less developed country specializing in ordinary goods produced at lower cost should both benefit from mutual trade. This mechanism should force workers in uncompetitive industries to change to competitive ones in both countries and thus stimulate export and growth in economy. The intention and philosophy of, e.g., GATT seems to fit this pattern and the postulated result should then be growth and increased wealth worldwide. This is certainly true for the rich nations such as the United States, EU, and Japan. It could also be true for Southeast Asia, China, and some countries in South America. Furthermore, can the multifiber agreement benefit countries that export textiles, as is the case for India and Ghana, well known for their cotton cloth?

But there are serious obstacles to be reckoned with. The first is that a country with no or noncompetitive production and exports will be a born loser. This applies to most countries in Africa and some in South Asia and South America, many of which are among the poorest in the world. These countries will certainly decline into further poverty. Furthermore, the new strict antidumping rules will lead to exclusion of import of their goods to the developed countries and the protection of patents and origin will reduce the export of so-called "copy" products from the poor countries and in addition make vital imports of new seed and plants extremely expensive.

The next problem, which I have already mentioned, is even more serious. That is the more farsighted consequence of unselective growth. A production managed by the forces of market mechanism is unacceptable and irresponsible facing the combination of the fast growth of world population combined with limited resources. There are two obvious reasons for this fact. In the first place, there will be no resources for a rise in standard of living for all humans in just a few decades from now, and second, the market mechanism is unselective in the regulation of production. The only regulatory parameter is demand. This means that useful and highly necessary goods are produced alongside with, e.g., totally useless plastic products or even harmful merchandise, for example, most of the arms production. The last products mentioned waste precious raw materials and energy.

These facts are certainly realized by many officials in the United Nations, IMF, and WB, and I guess that there are several reasons for their low action level. For one thing the political management is forced to act shortsighted to be reelected. The dominating materialistic views have the effect that few are willing to see a reduction in the standard of living, even if it benefits their grandchildren. Furthermore, at present some people in the Western world are opposed to people of different races or colors, and in some countries fanaticism and religious fundamentalism are sad facts to reckon with. A further reason is that the recommendations of the "experts" seem to work so well here and now, so the public doesn't know, or maybe doesn't care, what to do to prevent the catastrophic consequences later.

Some might have the fatalistic view that solutions to problems decades ahead are irrelevant, as it is impossible for us to predict the future with any degree of certainty.

Chapter 5
Religion and the Poor

For what will it profit a man if he gains the whole world, and loses his own soul?

—Mark 8:36

Are there any obstacles in religion toward an increase and radical change of the aid system? If so, this is of major importance, as religious views pervade our feelings and attitudes, even if we are secularized in our everyday life. I shall briefly refer to some conditions that relate to our present subject.

As for Christianity, we have in the New Testament, as you certainly know, several words of Jesus regarding consumption and the poor. For example, in "The Gospel according to Matthew" we find in chapter 6: "Do not lay up for yourselves treasures on earth, where moth and rust destroy and where thieves break in and steal" (verse 19); "No one can serve two masters; for either he will hate the one and love the other, or else he will be loyal to the one and despise the other. You cannot serve God and mammon" (verse 24); and "Therefore I say to you, do not worry about your life, what you will eat or what you will drink; nor about your body, what you will put on. Is not life more than food and the body more than clothing?" (verse 25). I see this as a clear statement that you shall not collect wealth for yourself and that you cannot serve money if you serve God. You have to find other values in life than money and material goods and "hardware." In chapter 10 we find: "Provide neither gold nor silver nor copper in your money belts, nor bag for your journey, nor two tunics, nor sandals, nor staffs; for a worker is worthy of his food" (verses 9–10). This statement says that you shall not keep more money or material goods than you need, but you have a right to work for your necessary daily outcome (food). Then we have the famous story about the rich man from chapter 19: Jesus said to him, "If you want to be perfect, go, sell what you have and give to the poor, and you will have treasure in heaven; and come, follow Me" (verse 21). I think that these words speak for themselves.

In Acts we read in chapter 2: "Now all who believed were together, and had all things in common, and sold their possessions and goods, and divided them among all, as anyone had need" (verses 44–45). To give to the poor is a true Christian virtue.

In Buddhism, essential for a Bodhisattva, i.e., follower of the Lord Buddha, are the ten Paramitas, or rules of virtue, which have to be followed. I shall not consider the meaning of them all, but two of them have a special significance. These are Dana and Metta.

Dana is a spirit of self-sacrifice. This means that you must be munificent to all human beings. In an ancient legend of Buddhism we find the account of a woman who in order to keep the rule of Dana gave her children to another person. This of course has to be understood on a symbolic rather than literal level, indicating that you must be willing to give to others even those that are precious to you.

In Dharmapada, a statement of Buddhist rules, Metta is "infinite love to all human beings to the same degree as the love of a mother to her only son." The Buddha himself said that Metta must be "like a mother risking her life for the sake of her only child." It is said in addition that this is a kind of love that cannot distinguish between people; you have to love every single individual even if you have no sympathy for that individual. According to the traditional Buddhist scripts, the feeling should be deliberately practiced, beginning with a single object and gradually increasing until the whole world is suffused with such kinds of feeling.

I feel that these statements are as strong in formulation as the Christian ones and that they thus give an ideal starting point for aid to the poor in our world.

As for Islam, the matter is a bit more complicated. I have made a thorough study of the Koran and several other relevant scripts of Islam. *Zakaat* is mentioned in twenty places in the Koran. *Zakaat* is a yearly tax that all Muslims who are healthy and free of debt have to pay from their savings in order to help the poor. *Zakaat* purifies our possessions to show that we are not greedy, just as *Salaat* purifies our bodies and souls. The basis of calculation is belongings made of gold and silver or cash owned more than twelve months, all income from cattle or agriculture, and profits from production or industry.

Nisab is the minimum savings one must obtain in order to pay *Zakaat*, that is, 85 grams of gold and 595 grams of silver (or the same amount in cash) in one year. *Zakaat* is then calculated as 2.5 percent of the savings.

Zakaat is not and can never be a part of the common tax system. It is a matter between God and each believer (each Muslim). Only in a few Muslim nations is it allowed to draw *Zakaat* from the savings account.

But who should or could receive the money? The nearest relatives can certainly not receive one's *Zakaat*. Traditionally *Zakaat* is given to the poor, to people who ran into large debt, to the unemployed, and to people who suffer because of conversion to Islam. Typically it is to people from one's own society or country. There do not seem to be any traditions for donation of *Zakaat* to poor foreign countries, apart from infrequent sole donations from an Arabian prince or king.

I have made a study of different sects of Hinduism but,

unfortunately, with no conclusive result. My starting point was that Hinduism might be important as potentially up to 1 billion people are Hindus. On the other hand, most of them live in India, which is not expected to give major aid to POCs.

In the Avatara teachings of Vishnuism not much relating to our problem was found. The same was the case in Shiva teachings of the goddess Durga, Kali, or Ganesha.

Among the three well-known roads to salvation in Hinduism, Bhaktimarga, Inanamarga, and Karmamarga, the last mentioned may be the most promising for the present purpose. Very briefly, Karmamarga comprises actions (karma) that are marked by an act of sacrifice. The purpose of sacrifice is to turn destiny into a happy future in life or after death and ultimately to be liberated from *samsara* ("suffering") caused by karma in order to be united with the highest principle, i.e., Brahma. I shall not go into the Upanishads and the philosophical writings of Hinduism but point out that the sacrifice most often is food, flowers, or fruit disposed in front of the god or the holy principle. More seldom the sacrifice can be an animal, e.g., a goat. I have been talking to influential Hindus but have not been able to trace any major tradition of, as an act of sacrifice, donating to the poor and especially in other countries.

My conclusion concerning religion and the poor is that a tradition to give is found in Christianity and in Buddhism and thus in countries dominated by these religions. It is especially remarkable in Buddhism and seems to be a completely novel trait added to Hinduism by Buddha.

As for Islam and Hinduism, this tradition is somewhat incalculable in this connection, seen apart from the immense difference in the nature and philosophy of these religions.

The Muslims seem most inclined to give to other Muslims and may thus aid poor countries dominated by Islam. Their efforts can thus be directed to nations and regions populated by Muslims in need ("brother countries").

With respect to Hinduism, I have found no tradition to be immediately linked to alleviation of poverty. Here poverty seems to be a destiny.

I have here only touched the principal sides of the religious concepts. I am aware that attitudes are not always in accordance with these concepts. Furthermore, it is obvious that fundamentalism and fanaticism can change matters markedly. In spite of these facts, I don't feel obliged to give a more complete description of these subjects, as they don't seem to be of major importance in this context.

A Global Ethic

In the fall of 1993 the Council of the Parliament of the World Religions arranged a congress in Chicago. The purpose was to agree on a Declaration toward a Global Ethic, and the participants represented forty-five different churches and religions, dominated by Christianity but with representatives from Hinduism and Buddhism.

The concept was worked out by the German Catholic theologian Hans Küng and the declaration contains, after a description of the global crisis, suggestions for solutions in four parts. In the first part it is stated that it is impossible to obtain a new global order without a global ethic enforcing responsibility on all humans. In the second part it is emphasized that each human being shall be valued equally everywhere in the world. In the third part the four basic rules common to all religions are stated, i.e., thou shall not kill; thou shall not steal; thou shall not lie; and thou shall not commit adultery. These should be understood as respect for human rights, nonviolence, respect for animals and plants, respect for other people, fair economic world order, elimination of poverty, misery, and misuse of the environment, a modest lifestyle, tolerance, a life of truthfulness, equal rights for all humans and between sexes, avoidance of infringement against children, and respect for matrimony and for celibacy in the tradition of various religions. In the fourth and last part each religious community was requested to formulate an ethic based on its own faith that would lead to a "conversion of the heart." The declaration is based on the philosophy that the religions are the foundation of ethics and that ethical responsibility should rest within the attitude of each human.

The statements of the declaration are of a kind no one can disagree with, but I certainly have a strong feeling that it shall be difficult to take further steps towards a solution of the problems of poverty and misery and a universal recognition of equal rights of each human without a framework, a novel economic responsibility to the poorest, and an organization with the authority and power to enforce the actions necessary for this purpose.

Chapter 6
Be Twins

There are two kinds of happiness, O monks; the happiness of the householder and the happiness of the ascetic. But the greater of the two is the happiness of the ascetic.
—Anguttara-Nikaya, Duka-Nipata

As stated in chapter 3, the main challenge is to unify an industrialized and an agrarian economy. The starting points are as different as possible.

In the EU the experts talk about bringing the economies of Eastern Europe "up to a level" of the West in order to let these countries enter the EU. They must "qualify"—they have to achieve a certain "standard" before this can happen.

A basic condition of the idea of twin formation is the introduction of a significant modification in the arbitrary market mechanism, multinational company, and business–managed world scenario. As previously mentioned, it seems obvious that we can't afford this kind of future development because of the novel situation of exponential population growth, exhaustion of precious raw materials and energy for partly useless production, extinction of species, and pollution from, e.g., superfluous consumption.

There are thus principally at least two possible ways that the world can follow from now on. The way that we see at present which will result in an arbitrary selection of an array of rich and poor nations, with slow and late action to improve the environment. We shall certainly see lots of commissions and reports, but little will be done because the real power is unmanaged business and profit.

Second is the twin way, where in principle each "poor" nation has a "rich" partner to secure equality in welfare and a common responsibility in the use of resources of all kinds. This will mean increasing equality and environmental responsibility worldwide between the poorest and the richest because no nation will be "lost" in poverty. Furthermore, decrease in population growth will result from an increase in welfare and education in the POCs of South America, Africa, and parts of Asia.

This also means stopping the present "aid model," where each rich nation sprinkles a bit of sugar on a number of selected partners, up to now with a result of increased poverty over the last thirty years. Each year we have patiently listened to statements from various government officials of "improvement" and "progress."

The twin model is a new aspect for world order. This calls for a branch of economics that I have named Ethical Economics (ETEC). The object of ETEC is an economy that values nature, environment, ecology, and culture as parts integrated with the ordinary economic "hardware." ETEC has to be developed as a novel science with cooperation in a broad sense incorporating people from all parts of society. I deliberately use the word "people" and not "experts." Experts of different kinds, including economists, are of course necessary, but they should join as sources of information and not as actual decision makers. That has to be so because their knowledge might be trapped in a framework of tradition and I feel that novel thoughts are more likely to come from the outside. Experts are often like drivers able to follow side roads of the main road, but not to jump over the mountain to a new main road.

It is thus, unfortunately, not yet possible to give a description in detail of ETEC, as evaluation has to be done as a cooperative effort from a multiplicity of sources. ETEC, then, has to be a philosophy as well as an instrument.

Twins are in principle two nations, that is, a POC and a developed country, in a union, and this is what I have in mind with the twin model, in the strict sense.

First I urge the reader to understand that details in the following are my suggestions and as such only meant as examples of possible solutions. What is important is to grasp the idea of the twin model.

To be twins in the "twin model sense" means that two societies, e.g., nations, within an agreed period of time take responsibility for each other in order to secure equal welfare, education, social security, and equality of other parameters of society. The citizens of each of these societies shall be granted a certain amount of favors in the society of the twin—i.e., equal possibilities of education and social support—and the final goal is equality in all important sectors of society.

The two societies or nations must be of around the same population. It is, for example, an obvious absurdity to imagine Finland to be a twin with India. A world body as coordinator for selection of twin partners is desirable, and the United Nations might be a natural choice.

I would suggest that at least the fifteen to twenty-five poorest nations in the world be selected for twin economy and a number of the richest countries in the Western world with approximately equal populations placed at disposal as twin partners. In the United States several models could be possible. One may be that each state has its own partner or that a group of states shares partner(s). I am of course aware that a thorough review of laws and regulations of the union can be necessary for implementation of this procedure.

The twin model doesn't need to be confined to two societies; it can be applied to close cooperation or union of a small group of POCs and developed countries within the same management structure and frame of economy, i.e., based on ETEC.

The conception for the world order is that we in the twin period have two groups of "countries" in development, i.e., the twins, each consisting of a poor and a rich partner, and what could be called the "in-betweens," that is to say, a hundred nations or more, neither rich nor really poor, which should not be offered twin partners.

At the end of the twin period, after maybe forty to fifty years have passed, we will strive to have a situation of fair welfare and justice for world citizens based on enduring ecological principles. We will thus fulfill our long-overdue promise in the UN Declaration of Human Rights, article 25.1.

As stated, the twin model can use ETEC as an integrated basis for the buildup of the common sectors of community, but ETEC must be suited for operation in various contexts or combinations of economy as far as the condition is set for bilateral inequality as the starting position. In 1985 I published a manifesto for ETEC that I think still can be useful. (ETEC was called ETCOM at that time.) This manifesto includes:

1. Evaluation of material resources, e.g., raw material, industrial capacity, etc., for each twin party.
2. Evaluation of natural resources, e.g., forests, deserts, etc., for each twin party.
3. Evaluation of cultural resources of each kind in twin societies, e.g., resources of education, heritage, etc.
4. Evaluation of negative resources, e.g., pollution, energy-wasting activities, use of scarce raw materials in futile production, destructive activity and use of nature, for example forests.

These evaluations should be done in the initial phase in

both societies (e.g., countries) and be revised on a regular basis during the whole twin period.

The initial evaluation should be performed by a broad selection of citizens from both societies. Citizens from other nations can be allowed to be advisers on strict conditions, with no decision-making power whatsoever. Initial evaluation is fixed for a certain period, for example five years, with a possibility of an extension of three years.

Following the initial evaluation period an agreement between the parties based on its results should be the outset of the twin period. It is of importance that a full equality exists between the parties. Under no circumstances can the richer party dominate or dictate conditions. Here "richer" is used as a traditional conception. In the ETEC concept the POC partner can be the rich one.

By the twin period is understood the agreed span of years from the initial phase until the equality phase. I have rather arbitrarily suggested that period be maybe thirty to forty years. The ultimate decisions in the twin period will be made by the body that I have named the Twin Council. The Twin Council could be elected indirectly, i.e., by the individual parliaments of the countries and should of course have an equal number of members from the two parties (countries), for example 100 members from each. In the period of initial evaluation a listing of twin matters could be agreed upon and these should in the twin period be presented to the parliaments of both nations, but the final decision in matters of this kind has to be made by the Twin Council. In the rare cases where a decision isn't possible in the council, a Twin High Court may take the final decision.

After the twin period has come to an end, a looser cooperation between the former twins can eventually be agreed upon. This cooperation could favor citizens of both parties in matters of, e.g., education, science, and technology.

Opposed to economic growth in an unselective way, a growth in the twin societies under use of the ETEC concept is desirable.

A few practical hints concerning implementation of the ETEC way might be indicated even if they have to have the character of general statements.

ETEC must look for means to harness market forces that have to be embedded in political decision mechanisms. All spheres of public policy must be infused with environmental concerns; otherwise an overall environmental pressure beyond what the ecological buffers could stand can easily be the result.

It will be important to look into determinants of processes leading to uncontrolled economic growth as an unchecked force in (twin) society.

The policy must have means to bridge the gap in wealth between economies and manage the striving for profit and market control.

A political stability and security should be maintained to effect redistribution of common resources in a peaceful and accepted way.

Instruments and means to control tensions in societies should be developed in the initial evaluation period.

Labor-replacing technology has to be implemented gradually in order to secure the necessary adaptation of twin societies.

Intensive common research in technology to seek novel solutions in industry and agriculture in order to save raw materials and reduce pollution in a nonprofit way should be encouraged.

Long-term agreements between the political management and industrial and agricultural sectors of societies based on economic and environmental forecasting and planning can be necessary to alter the pattern of production and thus consumption in ways to level and secure basic welfare of citizens of both societies.

I have performed calculations on the ETEC concept according to, among others, modified Leontief methods with various initial conditions, vector patterns, and interdependencies. Some progress was made in the set-up of models, but it showed that the science of economics methodologically is still in a rather basic state when compared to, e.g., pure or applied physics. A result was that the procedures at present followed by the WB and the IMF may be useful for a stable population of about 4 billion people worldwide. As applied now it seems to be a "who comes first strategy," with the last ones stamped "disfiguration." That is like applying the WB-IMF strategy to Asia and the rich world of North America, Europe, and Australia, while the two continents of Africa and South America disappear in the oceans overnight. Is that what we want?

Corruption is a problem in certain African and Asian countries such as, for example, Kenya and Bangladesh. This of course has to be taken seriously and brought under control already in the phase of initial evaluation by means of regulations and direct contact to and cooperation with people in local communities, e.g., farmers and residents of the countryside. Ultimately, it is of importance to encourage a new understanding and attitude to welfare and a concept of "happiness" focused on human values, physical and psychical well-being, and certainly away from the close connection to wealth.

Concluding Remarks

In the last thirty years we have seen report after report at an ever-increasing rate. We have seen many words of warning and even more of compassion for the poor, for the environment, and for the globe.

Much time has been wasted along the well-known established course, but results have been sparse in spite of "aid" and "experts." The expert may go and take a look in a village in the daytime and go to a party in the international hotel at night. The next day, negotiations with big business and maybe fat cats and a millon-dollar project is in place for an industry to export plastic toys for children in France or perfume products for women in Switzerland. Business as usual, but it is really a pity for the people in the village. Maybe they shall manage tomorrow on a meal of salted rice and a roasted frog or snake.

This said, I am of course aware of the existence of organizations and people who contribute in valuable ways to better the lives of those who suffer from poverty and famine.

As for the twin concept, I want it to be understood and discussed as a combined solution of at least two major problems: first, as a system to obtain a fair state of welfare in the poorest countries of the world, and second, to guide the richest countries to a course of much more effective action and responsibility concerning the use of resources of raw materials and pollution not only locally but globally. This goal can't be reached by "growth" or the "free market" as the only means. These means have no discriminatory power apart from sorting out people and countries into rich and poor categories. For this purpose they are really successful.

You grow whether you produce guns, plastic toys, or tools for better agriculture. For lasting solutions, a novel kind of world order is needed, where it will be necessary to impair the free movement of capital and merchandise and where a mutual link is established between the richest and poorest countries, as in, e.g., the twin concept.

Close contact with another culture, friendships, and links between families in the twin societies is certainly most important for success. Each family could be encouraged to have a "friend family" in the twin society. To know each other is the best way to bring about warm feelings between people.

Select References

Ahmad, M. G. *Islam.* Ahmadiyya Islamic Movement, 1896.
Ayittey, G. B. N. Editorial, *Wall Street Journal,* March 1994.
Bongaarts, J. "Can the Growing Human Population Feed Itself?" *Scientific American,* March 1994.
Brown, L. R. (ed.) *State of the World.* Worldwatch Institute, Washington, D.C., 1991–94.
Chipenda, J. "Suspend the Demand for Democracy." *Magazine for International Christian Church Aid,* March 1993.
DanChurchAid Statement, March 1994.
Diehl, C. G. *Instrument and Purpose; Studies on Rites and Rituals in South India.* Lund, Sweden: Gleerup, 1956.
Farquhar, J. N. *Modern Religions Movements in India.* New York: Macmillan, 1913.
Feynman, R. P. *What Do You Care What Other People Think?* London: Unwin Hyman, 1988.
George, S. *A Fate Worse than Debt.* Middlesex, England: Penguin, 1988.
Grosvenor, G. M., W. Graves, and J. B. Garver. *Africa Threatened.* Washington, D.C.: National Geographic Society, 1990.
Grosvenor, G. M., W. Graves, and J. F. Shupe. *Communism to Capitalism.* Washington, D.C.: National Geographic Society, 1993.
Haavelsmo, T., and S. Hansen. Report, *Social Economy.* Oslo, March 1992.
Harrison, P. *Inside the Third World.* Middlesex, England: Penguin, 1987.

Heine, G. "A Global Ethic." *Journal of Human Rights*. Oslo: Scandinavian University Press, 1994.

Hvidtfeldt, A. *Buddhism*. Copenhagen: Politikens Forlag, 1982.

International Monetary Fund. *World Economic Outlook*. Washington, D.C., 1994.

Kennedy, P. *Preparing for the Twenty-first Century*. London: Harper Collins, 1993.

The Koran. London: Islam International Publications, 1989.

Mann, J. (head of board of directors). Report from the Francois-Xavier Pagnond Center for Health and Human Rights, presented at the Harvard School of Public Health, 1994.

Meadows, D. H., D. L. Meadows, and J. Randers. *Beyond the Limits*. U.K.: Chelsea Greer, 1992.

New King James Bible. London: Thomas Nelson, 1979.

Norwegian Research Council for Science and the Humanities. *Sustainable Development, Science and Policy*. Oslo, 1990.

Olsen, G. R. *Africa—The Indomitable Continent*. Copenhagen: D. R. Baggrundsserie, 1994.

Rasmussen, H. T., and N. *From Cape to Cairo: On Motorbikes across Africa*. Copenhagen: Gyldendal, 1994.

Renteln, A. D. *International Human Rights: Universalism versus Relativism*. Newbury Park, CA: SAGE, 1990.

Sachs, J. *Poland's Jump to the Market Economy*. U.K.: MIT Press, 1994.

Torture: Quarterly Journal on Rehabilitation of Torture Victims and Prevention of Torture. Copenhagen: International Rehabilitation Council for Torture Victims (IRCT), 1993–94.

Tuchsen, H. *A World of Difference*. Copenhagen: Berlingske Tidende, May 1993.

UNESCO (United Nations Educational, Scientific, and Cultural Organization). *World Science Report*. New York, 1994.

UNFPA (United Nations Population Fund). *The State of World Population*. New York, 1993–94.

White, P. T. "Rice: The Essential Harvest." *National Geographic Magazine,* May 1994.

Winternitz, M. *Geschicte der Indischen Litteratur 2*. Berlin: Litteratur Religiöser Wissenschaft, 1913.

World Bank. *World Development Report.* Washington, D.C., 1992–94.

World Commission on Environment and Development. *Our Common Future.* Oxford: Oxford University Press, 1987.

Ytsen, F. "Dollars Conquer Hanoi." *Weekendavisen* (Weekly News), Copenhagen, May 1994.

The Twin Foundation

The Twin Foundation is an independent institution founded in solidarity with the poorest people in the Third World in order to realize a true responsibility based on the twin principles.

If you sympathize with this view, you can feel sure that your help and support will be of great significance.

If you want to help, please send your contribution to:

>The Twin Foundation
>Den Norske Bank
>(The Norwegian Bank)
>N-6400 Molde
>Acc. no. 7435.66.14465